Chapter One

Sophie woke to a sea of black. She blinked numerous times, after that expanded familiar with the dark. Soon she was able to see a drip of moonlight infiltrating her home window. Overwhelmed, she browsed around for whatever had made her awaken.

She had actually forgotten to shut her curtains prior to bed, and there was one twinkling star caught in the window structure. Its light was so intense, it appeared as though the celebrity was looking down at her specially. Watching over her while she rested.

Such a creativity! That was what her mum used to state.

Sophie sighed, and also was about to turn over in bed when the sound of voices surprised her into a resting placement.

' Janet always did what was best for the woman, and also currently we have to do what is finest for her too,' Aunty Christine was saying, right outside her bedroom.

' Yet she's my child!' Daddy exclaimed angrily. 'You can't just take her away from me.'

' Keep your voice down, she'll hear us,' her auntie hissed.

' Sophie will be far better off with us, as well as you understand it.' It was her Uncle Daniel's deep voice, soothing her daddy's temper. 'You're not on your own at the moment, you're still grieving for Janet. Sophie requires convenience and security today. Not a negligent papa.'

' I'm not reckless,' Dad urged. 'Yes, I have actually missed out on choosing Sophie up from institution a few times lately, and also occasionally she's needed to make her very own tea. However I can not aid the hrs I'm informed to function, and also she enjoys to care for herself when I'm not around.' He sounded irritable. 'I'm doing what I can to support my family.'

' We'll come round tomorrow mid-day to take her away. I wish you will not combat us on this,' her aunt claimed silently. 'Please think us, we are not being harsh. We are doing the best for our niece until you are feeling much better.'

Sophie listened to Uncle Daniel and Aunty Christine's footprints relocating away, then a door knocked as they left the flat.

Dad stomped away to the living room and quickly she heard the audio of the tv.
Sophie lay back down in her bed, crying gently to herself. This was all due to her.
Wiping her eyes on her sleeve, she remembered the day her mum had actually died. She had strolled home with Mum after school as usual, telling her everything about her buddies. After tea, Dad had gone upstairs to check out, while Mum had taken Sophie outside to consider the stars due to the fact that it was a clear evening.
' Shall we go to the park?' Mum had asked. 'We might get a much better view of the celebrities from there.'
They will go across the roadway to the park opposite when Sophie avoided ahead. Not looking both methods and listening for traffic as she had actually been educated, she ran right off the sidewalk equally as a cars and truck came shrilling round the bend.

Mother shrieked her name and also pressed Sophie out of the way. However she was struck by the auto herself.
Fresh splits developed in Sophie's eyes as she bore in mind informing her tale to the policeman afterwards. The cars and truck's chauffeur had driven away at top speed, but Sophie took care of to bear in mind part of his number plate as well as tell the police.

Over the past couple of months, Father had actually been required to offer their residence and also rent out a little and wet level, because they no more had the money from Mum's task. And Sophie had shed all her friends, as it was her very first year at a new college in a new location.

After overhearing Papa's disagreement with her aunt and uncle, Sophie strove but might not get back to sleep. In the long run, she switched the light on and also check out a book rather, expecting the first drip of sunup on the horizon outside. By the time she ended up guide, the bleak, cloud- cluttered sky was virtually light. At least it was a weekend break, she thought with relief, and she

did not need to struggle through a complete school day.
She switched off her light, and left the space.
She waltzed with the living room to the kitchen area, where she put on the kettle. Considering that her mum's fatality she had actually found out to do many small tasks round your home herself, and also her tea-making was getting respectable. She reached up to the high cabinet for two cups, and began to prepare tea for them both as she heard her papa's sleepy footprints coming through the living room.
' Hi, Dad!' she claimed, attempting to act typical. She did not desire him to recognize that she had overheard his conversation last night.
' Hi, sproglet,' he replied gladly, ruffling her hair. He took his mug of tea. 'Thanks! You're up early.'
She sipped her tea. It was still extremely hot. 'Couldn't sleep. So what are we doing today?'
' I assumed we might most likely to the park, and afterwards ...' He thought twice. 'After that you might go to Aunty Christine and Uncle Daniel. They 'd like you to stick with them for a month or more. Due to the fact that you seldom get to see them, you understand?'

She still claimed not to understand the fact.
' However it's nearly Xmas. Why do I have to go with them? I do not even like them that much!'
' I'll visit every weekend break, as well as for Christmas. Perhaps you can also come here for a few hours on Christmas Day. They intend to make certain you're succeeding at college and obtaining your meals promptly.'

' I do not understand.'

Dad shrugged, looking embarrassed. 'Well, to be truthful, they assume I'm not myself at the moment - not true, by the way - yet as soon as I have actually obtained every little thing ironed out, you'll come back to deal with me.'
Sophie frowned, but did not bother saying with him. It seemed like everyone had actually made their minds up without consulting her. Customarily!
After completing her tea, she rinsed her mug while Dad was consuming his breakfast. But she was not satisfied.
Dad sighed, seeing her expression. 'It's hard, Soph, I recognize. But perhaps

they're right and also this is for the very best.'
' I do not see what's so incorrect with the means we live.'
He checked out at the damp flat. The wallpaper looked mouldy and was removing the walls. 'It's not a wonderful place for a kid to live though, is it? Anyhow, we're going to have our lunch in the park today, which I really hope will certainly cheer you up.' He placed his empty cup down close to the sink and also threw an arm concerning her shoulders. 'You like the park.'
' It's a little bit cool for an outing,' she said, unsure.
' We'll conclude well,' he firmly insisted. 'Come on, you as well as Mum were constantly going to the park together.'
' So what are we bringing?' Sophie asked, reversing with an authentic smile on her face. She did not want Father to assume he was not as close to her as Mum had been. 'Maybe we can take a plastic sheet to put under the picnic covering. In case it's wet.'
' Just like your mum, you consider every little thing! Though we could just remain on a picnic bench.'
' Grim,' she claimed, and also claimed to tremble. 'It's not an appropriate barbecue unless you rest on the yard.'
He chuckled. 'Okay, I assumed we could bring some jam sandwiches, as well as a.

container of pop, as well as ... a few other barbecue points that I have no real idea what they are?' he added comically, making Sophie laugh.
' I think this is mosting likely to be my call, huh?' 'Yeah, I guess so.'.
Sophie got going on the food. It was a bleak day to have a barbecue in the park, but that cared? She was mosting likely to be living away from Father for time, by the sound of it. She might as well enjoy on their last day together. Something to remember when she was sitting lonely as well as burnt out at her aunt and also uncle's residence miles away in the country.
Once she was done making the sandwiches, she discovered that Papa had put in the time to discover a beautiful covering for them to remain on, together with some warm garments.

As Sophie obtained altered, her mind strayed back to her mum. Was she viewing her from heaven currently, happy with her daughter, or was she angry at exactly how badly things were going? Was her mother ashamed of her?

Splits started to develop in her eyes as she thought of just how disappointed her mum might be, enjoying from heaven.

' You prepared, sproglet?' Daddy asked cheerfully, knocking on her bed room door as well as snapping her back to reality.
' Yeah!' she replied, fast cleaning away her splits. 'Hold on. Simply a min!'. She was grinning once again by the time she unlocked.
There stood Dad. He had grass-green eyes, just like Sophie herself. He had brownish hair though, unlike Sophie's wonderful ginger, which she received from her mum. He was using a green V-neck coat and a dark brown coat over the top, and also was bring the hamper of food in his arms.
' Wow!' she exclaimed, staring at the hamper. 'Looks like I made rather too much food just for the two of us!'.

' So we'll feed the birds and squirrels.' He smiled. 'Come on!'.
Sophie rolled up the blanket he had found them, as well as folded it to fit in her knapsack. She turned it over her shoulders, responded to Papa that she was ready, as well as they triggered.
Papa secured the flat door behind them and slid the type in his pocket. They walked across the dank hall to the rustic old lift. As the doors moved closed, Sophie pressed G for the very beginning, after that cleaned her edge in the plain reflective wall of the lift.
As they left the block of apartments, Sophie examined her watch. It was almost lunch-time, and a five-minute walk throughout the park to the picnic location. She was grinning, yet in her head she was counting down the minutes to when she would certainly be separated from her daddy.

They stopped a brief means from the kerb and also looked both methods for traffic prior to going across the roadway. Sophie considered her mum regretfully, and also the awful crash that had taken her away permanently. But she maintained smiling. Mum died to save me, she assumed. I do not wish to let that sacrifice go to waste.

They treked through the tall iron entrances of the park as well as took the primary path with the middle. There were children's swings and climbing up frames to one side, however they transformed left halfway across towards the barbecue benches. It was quieter than the play area, however much greener as well, with even more trees and also shrubs.

Sophie smiled. She liked nature. She can even hear a couple of birds in the high branches of the trees.
' I'll set up the plastic sheet and blanket. You go and discover,' Daddy told her.
She responded, as well as questioned off to a pebbly area under some trees. It was extremely tranquil there. She was getting a round white stone when she froze, seeing something unexpected.
In front of her, on the other side of the pebbly area, stood a young puppy. It was.

cute! Sunset-ginger with charming huge paws also large for the rest of its body, a wagging tail and long, drooping ears. Its eyes were soft hazel and also extremely broad, staring at her.
The two stood motionless, staring at each other in amazement. Then Sophie dropped her stone with a loud smashing. The young puppy backed away, possibly surprised by the noise, then ran off into the trees.
' Wait, puppy!' Sophie chased after it.
She virtually caught up with it. But after that the puppy eluded behind a big tree. When she looked round the large trunk, the young puppy had not been there. She looked all over however there was no sign of the ginger puppy.
It was as if the pup had just gone away.
Sophie hurried back to the pebbly area, frowning. She has to have been gone ages as well as Daddy would be beginning to stress. She really did not want that.
Luckily, he was only just starting to look for her when she emerged from the trees. She did not discuss the vanishing puppy. He most likely had sufficient on his mind already.
Holding her father's hand, she wandered back to the barbecue location with him. 'This looks fantastic!' she said loudly, muffling the blanket and also appreciating Father's abilities at laying out the food.
' Well, I simply put everything out on the covering. You're the one that made it.'.

She hesitated over what to consume first. 'It does smell great.'.

' And also it's tasty as well! Well done,' Father claimed, taking another bite out of the jam sandwich she had created him.
Sophie blushed at the compliment. 'Thanks, Father. It was a wonderful suggestion to come out for an outing, even if it is a bit chilly!
Father grinned. 'Your mother loved outings too. Actually, I brought her right here as soon as for our wedding anniversary ...' He stopped quickly, understanding what.

he had said.
' It's all right, Papa. I don't mind you discussing Mum,' she assured him.
He nodded. 'Okay. However just if you make sure?' he asked. 'I do not intend to disturb you.'.
' It is very important that we talk about her.' Sophie provided him a weak smile.
' Oh darling.' Daddy brought her right into a cozy hug. She let tears freely drop her cheeks, as well as her eyes obscured.
' It's my whole fault that she died, Father! All my fault,' she sobbed. 'No, it isn't. Hush, it's alright, Sophie.'.
' But that car ... If I hadn't face the road so unreasonably.'.
He let her out of the hug and also cleaned away her splits. 'It will certainly never be your mistake. 'Your mother would not desire you to blame on your own. Believe me on this.'.
He kissed her on the forehead tenderly. After that she heard him rustle in his pocket. He highlighted a chocolate bar.
' Delicious chocolate makes everything better.' Father unpacked the delicious chocolate bar, as well as gave it to her.
Sophie took a few bites, and also started to feel far better. Yet there was one point dragging her down. 'However Daddy, it is my fault,' she said miserably. 'I ran ahead when I must have waited for Mum, and I didn't look appropriately when I crossed the road. I ought to have been the one who died, not her!'.
' Never ever claim that. That is one of the most false point you have actually ever said. You were not expected to die. If you had, after that ...'.
There was a moment of full silence between them. 'I'm sorry, Dad.'.

' Let's not consider the past, but the future.' Daddy handled a smile, and she knew he was being endure for her. 'Come on, what did you see when you went discovering?'.

' I saw a pup,' she started enthusiastically. 'A really charming pup. But when I moved, it ran. I tried to select it up, but it hid behind a tree.' She drank her head, remembering. 'It was really weird, really. When I looked behind the tree, the young puppy had actually vanished into thin air!'.
' Wow, that does seem strange. What kind of puppy was it?'.
' Oh, it was lovely! It had a waggy tail, and really charming extra-large paws, two times as big as its head,' Sophie told him, grinning. 'It was gingerish yellow like a sundown, as well as had large floppy ears. The cutest young puppy ever!'.
It was incredible just how conveniently the discussion had changed. She started to explain the puppy, and felt a cozy, fuzzy sensation inside. As if simply discussing the young puppy had altered everything. For the very first time in the past month or two, she felt happy once again.
' I just hope it's not lost,' she added, instantly stressed.
' I make sure it just strayed from its owner for a couple of minutes, that's all,' Dad guaranteed her. 'That's where the pup disappeared to, I expect. It didn't disappear, it returned to its owner.'.
She nodded gladly.

After a bit, the discussion altered from the pup to dog breeds, then felines, after that their old senior neighbours that had loads of pet cats. Sophie loved talking with her father, he was constantly so delighted to chat regarding pets.
' What's the moment?' Sophie asked unexpectedly.
Papa eyed his mobile phone. 'Two o'clock already!' He made a face. 'Well, we have actually consumed all the food, so I guess the picnic's over. Your auntie as well as uncle will certainly be waiting. Come on, aid me evacuate. We had much better be coming back.'.

They evacuated the barbecue, and left the park. Sophie padded silently alongside Dad as they made their way residence. However completely her head was turning left as well as right, on the look-out for an adorable ginger young puppy.

However there was no indicator of her little pal. Dad was right. The young puppy had probably gone back to its proprietor currently.
When they arrived home, the block of flats was quiet. The majority of individuals living there were out at institution or job, she presumed. They rose in the rustic, lonely lift to the fifteenth flooring, where they trudged throughout the dank, dark hallway.

This was the cheapest place to live in community, her dad had actually informed her as soon as. And forever factor!
In their level, Sophie went straight into the kitchen area and also threw away the remains of their outing. She folded up the tartan barbecue covering, put it back in the cabinet, after that went to see what her papa was doing.
But when she got involved in the living room Papa was standing at the door, talking to somebody in the corridor.
' Papa, that is that?' she asked him. She looked previous him at the site visitors. It was Aunty Christine as well as Uncle Daniel. They were standing in the doorway, disapprove their faces. Aunty Christine's white-blonde hair was in a braid, and she was using a red jumper.
Uncle Daniel had dark brownish hair and also blue eyes. He used a coat zoomed- approximately his neck as well as was bring a huge empty bag. She did not think he looked really friendly.
' Hello there, Sophie! We've concerned take you to cope with us awhile. The bag is for your things. We can come back later for even more of it if you like.'.
Sophie responded, took the large bag to her bedroom, and also began to load it up with fundamentals. Not simply clothing as well as shoes she would need, and some.

things from the bathroom, however her favourite publications and soft playthings too. Once it was full, she lugged it back to Uncle Daniel. The bag was really heavy as well as banged against her leg.
All 4 of them went down in the lift. It was even chillier outside currently, and also the skies looked extremely gloomy.
Sophie stopped as she will get involved in her aunt as well as uncle's silver vehicle. She offered Daddy a warm hug as well as did not wish to release. Her eyes endangered to splash rips, however she held them back. It would just upset him if he saw her sobbing.

Dad kissed her on the forehead. 'I'll see you quickly. Believe me, sproglet.'

'Bye, Dad,' she murmured.
Sophie felt her tears circulation at the label. Yet he was visiting her quickly. He had promised.
She cleaned the rips away, and also climbed up inside the car.
As her uncle repelled, she saw Dad waving bye-bye. He was grinning, however she could tell he was sad inside.
' I will not criticize you if you weep. You aren't going to see him at Christmas or New Year,' Aunty Christine told her coldly from the guest seat.
' But I believed Father was involving go to soon!'.
' I'm sorry, but you aren't going to see him till he sorts himself out. Which will certainly take some time.' Uncle Daniel checked out her in the mirror as he drove the auto. 'It could be months before that takes place.'.
She really felt the tears roll down her cheeks, as well as this moment not did anything to quit them. All she might consider was her Papa.
Would certainly she ever see him once again?
Uncle Daniel drove for concerning a hr, out of town and also into the countryside. The journey seemed to go on permanently. But at last it was over.

and the cars and truck gradually pulled up.
Exhausted as well as bored, Sophie climbed out of the silver vehicle and extended, yawning. She studied the little home in front of her. It was bordered by a big yard with a fishpond and a shed. Ivy holds on to the cream- coloured wall surfaces of the house. There were fields stretching all over them in every direction.
It looked like a pleasant, countryside home. However to Sophie it was a prison.
Aunty Christine smiled and also unlocked the front door. 'Welcome to your brand-new house.'.

Chapter 2

Sophie felt unpleasant in the juvenile new garments Aunty Christine had demanded buying her. At the very least she would not know anyone here, she advised herself. Considering that her old park was an hour away, she had to dip into the new neighborhood park. But if any individual saw her, they would certainly think she was a freak. Her jumper was scarlet, and also it combined terribly with her ginger hair.

She sighed and counted on take a look at Aunty Christine.

Her aunt's brownish hair looked colored, with grey touches in position. She was much older than Papa, and also was beginning to crease under her eyes. Her eyeshadow was a blue-turquoise, and she had huge fake eyelashes. Sophie attempted not to evaluate her aunt, however actually, she was horrible.

Aunty Christine held out a ring-encrusted hand. She had a smile on her face.

'Do you like your new garments?'

Sophie inwardly cringed. 'Um, yeah. Thank you a lot.' 'My pleasure, sweetie. They behave as well as brilliant, aren't they?'

That's for sure, Sophie believed with a grimace. Yet she did not tell her aunt the awful reality. It had actually been very type of her to get Sophie brand-new clothing whatsoever.

' Yes, they are. Do you think they fit me?' she asked nicely, giving up and also taking her auntie's hand.

' Oh, you look attractive in that jumper. Now come on, allow's go downstairs. We don't want to miss out on all the enjoyable.'

Sophie followed her downstairs hesitantly.

' Ooh, consider the moment! We have to be off, Sophie, or we'll be late. Let's go.'

Aunty Christine batted her fake eyelashes as they left the door throughout the crushed rock to the automobile.

It was a short drive to Sophie's brand-new neighborhood park. There were turning lanes that seemed deserted as Aunty Christine drove them along in the silver automobile.

As she rounded an edge, a sunset-ginger puppy with lengthy drooping ears suddenly ran in front of the car.
' Watch out!' Sophie screamed.
Aunty Christine slammed on the brakes, cursing under her breath. However there was no demand to quit the cars and truck. The young puppy ran right across the roadway without being hit. It was a wonder!
' Oh say thanks to benefits,' Sophie exclaimed, looking after it. 'I thought it was mosting likely to be eliminated. Silly young puppy! '
Aunty Christine opened her vehicle door as though ready to run after the pup. Yet when she went out and looked, there was no indicator of it anywhere.
' Exactly how very strange,' Aunty Christine said, hands on hips as she peered backwards and forwards the roadway. 'Where did that little doggy go? Did you see, Sophie?'
Sophie assumed she had actually seen 2 hazel eyes enjoying her through the hedge, but they were gone now. Probably just her creative imagination.
' No, Aunty.'

Yes, how strange, she believed also. That pup had looked much like the one she had seen in the park near Daddy's flat. However that was over a hr's drive away. It could not potentially be the same pup, she told herself.
When they reached the park her auntie was still troubled and also discombobulated, sputtering concerning proprietors that let their pups run about the road.

Sophie escaped as well as used the swings. It was quiet, only a few other youngsters playing in the park. None talked to her.
As soon as she got tired of being alone, Sophie rested on the park's meant 'friendship bench' in hope of drawing in a good friend. But the bench appeared

more to prevent aside from bring them better.
Bored, Sophie rose and tried to look for the barbecue location, but after wandering via the trees, she quickly realised she was lost. This park was much larger than the one she as well as Papa used to go to in town.
All of a sudden, backing away from a dark-looking part of the woods, she tripped over an obstacle on the ground as well as fell onto the turf.

' What currently?'
, she started to select herself up. Yet the obstacle was alive! It relocated as well as licked her face.
Sophie gasped.

It was a young puppy she had tipped over! A young puppy with acquainted ginger fur and soft hazel eyes. The pup checked out her quizzically.
' Hi, pup!' She was surprised, but stroked the downy hair on its head. 'You coincide dog I saw earlier, right? I do not know why you keep following me around. But you're extremely cute.'
The pup barked at Sophie's rumbling belly, as well as she laughed, a bit humiliated by the sound she was making.
' Sorry, I should be hungry!'
The puppy wagged its tail as if it understood what she was stating. 'I'm looking for the outing location, pup. I have actually never ever been to this park before. My aunt stated it was near the swings, however I can't keep in mind exactly how to get back to them.' Sophie put her directly one side, regarding the young puppy thoughtfully. 'Maybe you can assist me.'
The young puppy barked twice, after that competed off. 'Return below!' Sophie called after her.
As the pup slid between the trees, it appeared to disappear. Sophie

sighed, then hurried after it. 'Right here we go again ... '
She strolled as promptly as possible, complying with the strange flash of ginger through the trees in advance. Finally she located herself at the picnic area. One of the benches under the trees was not too moist. She looked about for the young puppy, however it had actually vanished once more. Shrugging, Sophie sat down and also drew her publication out of her pocket.
At least she might review below.

' Oh hi, Aunty Christine,' she claimed an instant later as her auntie approached her park bench.
Her aunt sat down and also looked at Sophie's publication. It was a Young Adult book concerning a dream land of witches as well as warlocks. It was an extremely exiting read, however her aunt frowned.

' Are you sure that appropriates for you to review, dear?' her auntie asked. 'I'm appreciating it.'
' Yet it's about witchcraft.'
Sophie merely made a face, as well as recalled at her publication. Her auntie sighed and wandered away, considering her smart phone.
When at last the phase was over, Sophie closed guide in a fanciful state, questioning what would occur following in the tale. She went back to the swings and took a seat, turning her feet. She got the cash her aunt had offered her for sugary foods, counted it, after that turned a little bit greater.
There was a tiny shop as well as cafeteria in the park. Sophie determined she would certainly have a great swing first, after that go as well as acquire some sweets before her auntie claimed it was time to go residence.
Instantly she listened to shouts as well as stomping feet behind her. She stopped turning and also turned around in surprise.

There were 3 teenage girls looking at her. One had actually dyed her hair red, the other environment-friendly, and also the last one had a puncturing in her nose, with a little silver ring.
' Provide us your cash, brat!' the one with red hair bought her aggressively.
' Yeah!' the other two chorused grimly.
' Yet I do not want to,' Sophie exclaimed, as well as propelled her cash back inside her layer pocket.

The green-haired one wheezed at her saucy reply, and the one with the nose-piercing grumbled like a dog.
Yet that was absolutely nothing. The tall one with red hair chose her up by the scruff of her neck, dragged her far from the swings and banged her versus a tree.
' Assist!'.
Sophie gasped for breath and had a hard time. Her head was throbbing and she wanted someone could save her, however nobody else was there.
Suddenly a menacing bark came from the other side of the course.
All three older girls relied on look, as well as the red-haired one released Sophie, who crumpled to the ground.
The bark returned, becoming a deep growl and also coming more detailed.
Sophie recognized that bark. She sought out at the ginger young puppy as the 3

women escaped.

' Thank you,' she managed to say weakly.
Still pushing the ground, Sophie jumped as the ginger puppy walked all over her, licking her face and also breathing on her warmly.
' Argh!' she cried, as well as pressed the animal away, chuckling. However when she had a hard time to her feet, once again the puppy had disappeared.

It was an enigma
Sophie sighed and slung her bag over her shoulder before treking to the shop and also cafeteria. She bought some desserts, and a drink of pop, and muffled a table all by herself.

She glimpsed around at the other people having their lunch there,. No one recalled at her. She asked yourself where her aunt had reached. Possibly she had actually obtained an important telephone call. Maybe from her father, saying he had actually obtained a better work and also flat, as well as prepared to have Sophie back residence with him.

That opportunity applauded her up, and she started to grin.
Sophie finished her lunch, then lcft the barbecue area as well as wandered around the park, trying to find her auntie. But she might not see her anywhere, and she can not remember now where they had parked the auto.

Depressing and lonesome, and a bit scared, Sophie ran to sit under an enormous old willow tree.
She sat underneath the sagging branches, attempting to stay out of view of every person, though the fallen leaves had all chosen winter season. The only light originated from an opening in the branches that beam coldly on her face.

Via it she can see the grey sky.
Sophie crossed her legs on the grass as well as pulled a picture out from her pocket. It was all scrunched-up and battered. Sophie unscrunched the picture as well as studied it.

The image had been handled the coastline throughout the summer vacations, prior to they had actually relocated below to go after Mum's job. Sophie's best friend Lily, Mum, Papa, Aunty Christine, Uncle Daniel and Sophie herself were all having a great time on the sand. Sophie looked at the picture of her mum's smiling face for a very long time.
She had actually inherited her mum's ginger hair. 'Like a sunset on your head,' Mum utilized to say, cuddling her.

A tear rolled down her cheek.
An unexpected bark made Sophie tear her gaze away from the photo to the bumpy origins of the tree. Down among the roots was a little hollow, instead like a rabbit hole, undoubtedly something that had actually been dug by its inhabitant. And the bark was coming from inside the hollow.
She did away with the image and also leaned over, peering into the hole. A pair of hazel eyes stared back at her, then she heard a soft whining.

It was the ginger puppy again. Hiding under the roots of the old willow tree.
' You!' she exclaimed, not able to believe her eyes.
The puppy barked noisally and also enthusiastically, breaking Sophie out of her puzzled thoughts.

' You're gorgeous,' she informed the young puppy, reaching in as well as snuggling its soft little body, 'therefore ginger. Much like me! I do wish you can discover your method house by yourself. However I need to get back to Aunty Christine, she has to be worried sick by now!'.
Sophie stood, and looked in all instructions. Where had Aunty Christine parked the cars and truck? She was hopelessly shed.

The puppy clambered out from under the crying willow's drooping branches, as well as cushioned away to the left, looking back over its shoulder at her.
' You desire me to follow you, young puppy?' The pup barked.
' Okay, but this had much better deserve it!'.
Sophie complied with the pup, needing to speed up as it began to bound across the lawn, and was soon short of breath.

The pup rounded an edge on the course and she skidded to a halt. Before her was a large gate to the roadway. And also there was Aunty Christine, waiting impatiently by her silver cars and truck.
Sophie glimpsed round, wondering where the puppy had gone. Yet there was no pup. It had actually possibly run back to its little den under the willow, she believed. She was sad to see it go, and wished it would certainly find its proprietor again soon. Yet Sophie recognized there was no factor informing her auntie regarding the strange puppy. She would just believe Sophie was making it approximately obtain interest!
Aunty Christine found Sophie and beckoned for her to hurry. She was on her phone, however ended up the call as Sophie came close to.
' It's all right, I have actually discovered her. I'll see you back at home, love,' she claimed into the phone, then shook her head at Sophie. 'Where have you been? I had to phone your uncle, I was so concerned. I believed you 'd escape!'.

Sophie moseyed across the road, looking and listening meticulously, and got involved in the vehicle.
' Hello, Aunty Christine!' She smiled at her aunt. 'Sorry, I lost track of time.'.
Her aunt looked frustrated, but got involved in the cars and truck as well.
'Well, at least you're back now. Put on your seatbelt.'.
Sophie pulled on her seat belt and also slung her bag onto the rear.
' I'm really sorry I kept you waiting. I went for a walk, after that could not locate my back to you. You recognize, a new park and all,' Sophie described as Aunty Christine began to drive home.

' I know that feeling!' Aunty Christine laughed, and also it seemed she was not mad anymore. 'I must have walked round it three times, seeking you. There were a few other children hanging round the swings, I discovered.' She eyed Sophie with any luck. 'Did you make any type of new pals?'.
Sophie thought of the three teenage girls. 'Um ...' she started to say, after that.

kept in mind the ginger puppy. 'Yes, I believe I might have done. However it's early days yet.'.
When they got back, Aunty Christine appeared extremely worn out. She really did not point out the near-miss mishap with the young puppy to Uncle Daniel,

so neither did Sophie. She obtained become her pyjamas, because it was currently dark.
She consumed tea with them in the kitchen area, sitting round the table. They were all quiet as she ended up and washed up her plate prior to going upstairs to bed.
Sophie rested on the edge of her bed as well as stared at the wall surface. She felt unpleasant. And also quickly it would certainly be Christmas.

Chapter Three.

' And also the winner of Strictly Come Ice Skating this year is Indifa, actor and also global popstar!' the speaker of the ice-skating show revealed, and also Indifa, in addition to her partner, skated towards her gracefully.
Indifa's comments were hushed by the joys of the group as she claimed the trophy: a set of golden ice-skates placed on a small gold platform. She was weeping satisfied tears.

Sophie sighed and also switched off the TV. She would certainly never have a possibility to be renowned, or win a prize like that for anything, let alone a glamorous sporting activity like ice skating. Aunty Christine and Uncle Daniel had gone upstairs early, so she was all alone.
She got up from the couch. Sad and exhausted, she roamed over to the Xmas tree. It really did not even be entitled to that title. It was a plastic environment-friendly tree with a couple of knickknacks. Under were three measly presents.

As well as it was Xmas Eve.
Sophie felt a tear run down her cheek.
She cleaned it away, and also glanced at her watch. 9 o'clock. She pulled on shoes and also a coat, as well as ran out into the night.
It was an over cast sky, as well as there was no moon, but the road was lit up with the white radiance of a little snow. She felt shivers gone through her body, and also blurt a breath which steamed on the chilly air. She chuckled, considering exactly how she and also her mom had actually constantly acted to be dragons in wintertime.
Sophie trotted down the country lanes, no regrets in her heart. Snow had been falling extra heavily on capitals; it thrived in small fractures on the covering of rich white. Crystal snowflakes flew from the paradises as well as froze the webs in the bushes.
Unexpectedly Sophie came to a fork in the roadway. One path led up to a field of.

snowy winter months wonderland, the various other down to an unsafe, icy ditch. She padded up in the direction of the area.

When she got to the gate, she can see a small village beyond with tiny houses, each roof glittering with snow.
Then she listened to a little whimper in the hedge. She crouched down and also pushed back some snow, prior to wheezing at the view.

' You once more!'.
A shuddering ginger young puppy with hazel eyes stared back at her. The charming little puppy jumped into her arms as well as yawned. Sophie felt herself destroying happily at the cuteness.
' Okay, dog, because you appear to wish to be with me, let's go.'.
Sophie grinned and began to climb over eviction to the field. However before she was fully over, the puppy slipped from her grip, leapt down as well as bounded away.

Sophie raced after the little dog throughout the field. It led her over a thorny hedge, throughout an icy lane, with a field with a cranky bull in it (that really did not finish well!), and also right into the town she had actually seen earlier.

Right here the puppy reduced, and she slipped after it through the town. She did not want anyone to see her and also call her auntie and also uncle. But once they were out of the town, the chase began again.
Down roadways, through areas, over livestock grids. For hrs she kept running up until all of a sudden the pup quit beside a car with its lights on, as well as barked.

It was a police vehicle. 'Hello,' the police woman claimed, frowning at Sophie and afterwards the young puppy. 'That's a stunning young puppy. However you two look lost. Where do you live?'.
Sophie bit her lip, then crossed her fingers and also gave the police woman her father's address.

On the drive home, the police woman asked her great deals of inquiries and also she answered them as honestly as she could. However she did tell a little white lie, saying the pup was hers.
' What's her name?'.
Was it a woman young puppy? Sophie grinned as well as had a fast peek prior to answering. Yes, it was a girl.

' Tinsel,' she said quickly. 'Her name's Tinsel.' The puppy grumbled and wagged its tail.
' That's extremely Christmassy.'.
' Oh, we love Xmas at my home,' she claimed happily. 'Me as well as my mum and daddy. Though ... my mum's gone now.'.
' Gone?'.
Silently, Sophie explained concerning the mishap.
' I'm so sorry,' the police woman stated affectionately. 'Yet I anticipate your puppy is a convenience right now of year.'.
' Yes,' Sophie agreed, embracing the cozy little body versus her. 'She actually is a comfort.'.
At the block of apartments, Papa opened the door. He appeared stunned at first to see a police woman on his front door. But then his face brightened when he saw Sophie, and also he pulled her right into a limited hug.
' Soph!' He squeezed her tight, drinking his head. 'You shouldn't have actually fled, you understand. Your auntie as well as uncle have actually been on the

phone every ten minutes, asking if you would certainly come below or sounded me.'.
' I'm sorry, Dad,' she whispered, virtually in rips. 'Aunty Christine as well as Uncle Daniel have actually been really kind to me. But I couldn't invest Xmas with them. This is my real residence. This is where I belong. With you.'.

The dog suddenly whimpered to leap down. Dad let Sophie go, as well as the puppy cushioned eagerly concerning the studio apartment.
Daddy stared at the puppy, stunned. 'Whose canine is that, Sophie? Did Aunty Christine obtain you a pup?'.
' , no ... I sort of discovered her.'.
He grinned, ruffling her hair. 'Count on you to find a puppy the very same colour as your hair. She looks much like you!'.
Just like me and also mum, she believed, however smiled back.

Looking about herself, Sophie became aware that her father had been hectic considering that she had actually left. He had remodelled the flat: brand-new wallpaper, fresh paint, as well as a brand-new cooking area table with 4 smart chairs. And also she might see from the paperwork on the cooking area table that he had actually obtained a brand-new job in a workplace.

The police woman talked with Dad for ages while Sophie played with the puppy, then she came by to bid farewell. 'It behaved to fulfill you and Tinsel, Sophie. Remain safe, yeah? Be sensible, and also no more running away!'.
Sophie responded. 'Thanks for bringing me residence.'.
The police woman smiled. 'Somebody will come round after Christmas to speak to you both. Yet it resembles you'll have the ability to return in with your dad. That's what you desire, isn't it?'.
' Greater than anything!'.
After the police woman had actually gone, Sophie took a look at her Father standing in the entrance and also really felt tears in her eyes. Memories of past Christmas Eves flooded right into her mind.
' I miss Mum so much.'.
' I recognize you do, Sophie.' He came and also embraced her, his voice close feeling. 'I miss her too. Currently we're back with each other, sproglet, I'm not going to let you go again. Your auntie as well as uncle had their opportunity.

But it's obvious.

you want to cope with me, not them.' 'I do, Dad. I actually do.'

' After that you shall,' he told her firmly, and kissed her on the forehead. 'I have actually obtained myself a proper work. And also I have actually been tidying up the level.'

' I recognize, it looks wonderful!'

' I have not revamped your room yet,' he admitted. 'But just due to the fact that I desire you to select your own wallpaper. As well as a brand-new bed.'

She can not quit grinning. 'I would certainly love that, Daddy. Thanks a lot.'

' I'm figured out to make this a comfy home for you,' he told her, nodding. 'Now come into the living-room. I've obtained a surprise for you.'

She followed him into the living room, uncertain what to expect.

It was a big Xmas tree. An actual Xmas tree. It had flashing lights twirled around pine-scented branches, glinting tinsel covered in between them, with red and gold knickknacks spicing it up. Underneath the tree were a load of vibrantly covered presents, all identified Merry Xmas, Sophie.

' Oh Father,' she murmured. 'It's fantastic!'

Extra tinsel had actually been strewn around the space, taped to the doors and window. All of it looked very festive as well as inviting. Yet there was something missing on the tree.

Daddy pressed something cold right into her hand. A gold star. She gasped and also he nodded. 'Take place,' he whispered. 'Your mom always did this little bit. However it's your turn now.'

Sophie stretched on tiptoe to repair the glittering star to the top of the tree, however it maintained diminishing.

' Below you go,' Dad chuckled, aiding her.

With each other they giggled as well as grinned. A Christmas never to be neglected

was only moments away.

The clock on the mantelpiece stated twelve o'clock at night. The neighborhood church bell begin to ring. Twelve chimes, and also she counted every one of them.

' Where's that young puppy gone?' Papa asked, glancing regarding with a frown.

' Tinsel? Tinsel?' Sophie called the adorable little puppy, walking around the level. She looked all over, even under her old bed. However the pup had actually vanished. Sophie really felt sad, yet not for long. 'I believe Tinsel was only below to bring us back with each other.'

Dad did not recognize, but seemed delighted simply to be back with Sophie. 'We're a household once more,' he said, and also embraced her. 'I do not understand just how. But it's a Christmas miracle.'

Sophie needed to agree. Though she wished that, any place the young puppy was, she was risk-free and delighted also.

' Merry Christmas, Sophie.' 'Merry Xmas, Father.'

Out in the cool night skies, a little spirit floated as much as sign up with the celebrities, and also a specific ginger pup went away for the last time, its final dream given.

Smiling gladly finally, Sophie sought out at the celebrities from the home window. And also Christmas Day began.

www.ingramcontent.com/pod-product-compliance
Lightning Source LLC
LaVergne TN
LVHW041307150826
845673LV00008B/2776

* 9 7 9 8 7 5 7 6 8 8 4 3 5 *